There is no need to forget your login details and passwords again! Simply write them down in this book to have them in easy reach when you need them.

There is room in the front of the book for your most-visited websites. Then you will find an A-Z listing with space for 16 websites for each letter. If you need extra space for any letter, use the spare pages at the back.

Make sure to keep the book safe and secure!

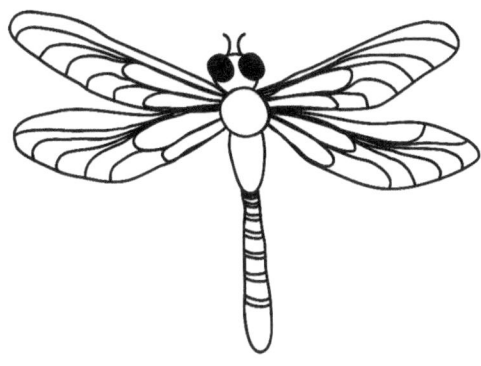

Website:

URL:

Username:

Password:

Notes:

Website:

URL:

Username:

Password:

Notes:

Website:

URL:

Username:

Password:

Notes:

Website:

URL:

Username:

Password:

Notes:

Website:

URL:

Username:

Password:

Notes:

Website:

URL:

Username:

Password:

Notes:

Website:

URL:

Username:

Password:

Notes:

Website:

URL:

Username:

Password:

Notes:

Website:
URL:
Username:
Password:
Notes:

Website:
URL:
Username:
Password:
Notes:

Website:
URL:
Username:
Password:
Notes:

Website:
URL:
Username:
Password:
Notes:

Website:
URL:
Username:
Password:
Notes:

Website:
URL:
Username:
Password:
Notes:

Website:
URL:
Username:
Password:
Notes:

Website:
URL:
Username:
Password:
Notes:

Website:

URL:

Username:

Password:

Notes:

Website:

URL:

Username:

Password:

Notes:

Website:

URL:

Username:

Password:

Notes:

Website:

URL:

Username:

Password:

Notes:

Website:

URL:

Username:

Password:

Notes:

Website:

URL:

Username:

Password:

Notes:

Website:

URL:

Username:

Password:

Notes:

Website:

URL:

Username:

Password:

Notes:

A

Website:
URL:
Username:
Password:
Notes:

Website:
URL:
Username:
Password:
Notes:

Website:
URL:
Username:
Password:
Notes:

Website:
URL:
Username:
Password:
Notes:

A

Website: _____
URL: _____
Username: _____
Password: _____
Notes: _____
_____
_____
_____

Website: _____
URL: _____
Username: _____
Password: _____
Notes: _____
_____
_____
_____

Website: _____
URL: _____
Username: _____
Password: _____
Notes: _____
_____
_____
_____

Website: _____
URL: _____
Username: _____
Password: _____
Notes: _____
_____
_____
_____

A

Website:

URL:

Username:

Password:

Notes:

Website:

URL:

Username:

Password:

Notes:

Website:

URL:

Username:

Password:

Notes:

Website:

URL:

Username:

Password:

Notes:

Website:

URL:

Username:

Password:

Notes:

Website:

URL:

Username:

Password:

Notes:

Website:

URL:

Username:

Password:

Notes:

Website:

URL:

Username:

Password:

Notes:

B

Website:

URL:

Username:

Password:

Notes:

Website:

URL:

Username:

Password:

Notes:

Website:

URL:

Username:

Password:

Notes:

Website:

URL:

Username:

Password:

Notes:

Website:

URL:

Username:

Password:

Notes:

Website:

URL:

Username:

Password:

Notes:

Website:

URL:

Username:

Password:

Notes:

Website:

URL:

Username:

Password:

Notes:

B

Website:
URL:
Username:
Password:
Notes:

Website:
URL:
Username:
Password:
Notes:

Website:
URL:
Username:
Password:
Notes:

Website:
URL:
Username:
Password:
Notes:

Website:

URL:

Username:

Password:

Notes:

Website:

URL:

Username:

Password:

Notes:

Website:

URL:

Username:

Password:

Notes:

Website:

URL:

Username:

Password:

Notes:

C

Website:

URL:

Username:

Password:

Notes:

Website:

URL:

Username:

Password:

Notes:

Website:

URL:

Username:

Password:

Notes:

Website:

URL:

Username:

Password:

Notes:

Website:

URL:

Username:

Password:

Notes:

Website:

URL:

Username:

Password:

Notes:

Website:

URL:

Username:

Password:

Notes:

Website:

URL:

Username:

Password:

Notes:

C

Website:

URL:

Username:

Password:

Notes:

Website:

URL:

Username:

Password:

Notes:

Website:

URL:

Username:

Password:

Notes:

Website:

URL:

Username:

Password:

Notes:

Website:

URL:

Username:

Password:

Notes:

Website:

URL:

Username:

Password:

Notes:

Website:

URL:

Username:

Password:

Notes:

Website:

URL:

Username:

Password:

Notes:

D

Website:

URL:

Username:

Password:

Notes:

Website:

URL:

Username:

Password:

Notes:

Website:

URL:

Username:

Password:

Notes:

Website:

URL:

Username:

Password:

Notes:

D

Website:
URL:
Username:
Password:
Notes:

Website:
URL:
Username:
Password:
Notes:

Website:
URL:
Username:
Password:
Notes:

Website:
URL:
Username:
Password:
Notes:

D

Website:
URL:
Username:
Password:
Notes:

Website:
URL:
Username:
Password:
Notes:

Website:
URL:
Username:
Password:
Notes:

Website:
URL:
Username:
Password:
Notes:

D

Website:
URL:
Username:
Password:
Notes:

Website:
URL:
Username:
Password:
Notes:

Website:
URL:
Username:
Password:
Notes:

Website:
URL:
Username:
Password:
Notes:

E

Website:
URL:
Username:
Password:
Notes:

Website:
URL:
Username:
Password:
Notes:

Website:
URL:
Username:
Password:
Notes:

Website:
URL:
Username:
Password:
Notes:

Website:

URL:

Username:

Password:

Notes:

Website:

URL:

Username:

Password:

Notes:

Website:

URL:

Username:

Password:

Notes:

Website:

URL:

Username:

Password:

Notes:

E

Website:
URL:
Username:
Password:
Notes:

Website:
URL:
Username:
Password:
Notes:

Website:
URL:
Username:
Password:
Notes:

Website:
URL:
Username:
Password:
Notes:

Website:

URL:

Username:

Password:

Notes:

E

Website:

URL:

Username:

Password:

Notes:

Website:

URL:

Username:

Password:

Notes:

Website:

URL:

Username:

Password:

Notes:

F

Website:

URL:

Username:

Password:

Notes:

Website:

URL:

Username:

Password:

Notes:

Website:

URL:

Username:

Password:

Notes:

Website:

URL:

Username:

Password:

Notes:

Website:

URL:

Username:

Password:

Notes:

F

Website:

URL:

Username:

Password:

Notes:

Website:

URL:

Username:

Password:

Notes:

Website:

URL:

Username:

Password:

Notes:

F

Website:
URL:
Username:
Password:
Notes:

Website:
URL:
Username:
Password:
Notes:

Website:
URL:
Username:
Password:
Notes:

Website:
URL:
Username:
Password:
Notes:

Website:

URL:

Username:

Password:

Notes:

Website:

URL:

Username:

Password:

Notes:

Website:

URL:

Username:

Password:

Notes:

Website:

URL:

Username:

Password:

Notes:

Website:

URL:

Username:

Password:

Notes:

G

Website:

URL:

Username:

Password:

Notes:

Website:

URL:

Username:

Password:

Notes:

Website:

URL:

Username:

Password:

Notes:

Website:

URL:

Username:

Password:

Notes:

G

Website:

URL:

Username:

Password:

Notes:

Website:

URL:

Username:

Password:

Notes:

Website:

URL:

Username:

Password:

Notes:

G

Website:

URL:

Username:

Password:

Notes:

Website:

URL:

Username:

Password:

Notes:

Website:

URL:

Username:

Password:

Notes:

Website:

URL:

Username:

Password:

Notes:

Website:

URL:

Username:

Password:

Notes:

Website:

URL:

Username:

Password:

Notes:

Website:

URL:

Username:

Password:

Notes:

Website:

URL:

Username:

Password:

Notes:

Website:

URL:

Username:

Password:

Notes:

H

Website:

URL:

Username:

Password:

Notes:

Website:

URL:

Username:

Password:

Notes:

Website:

URL:

Username:

Password:

Notes:

Website:

URL:

Username:

Password:

Notes:

Website:

URL:

Username:

Password:

Notes:

H

Website:

URL:

Username:

Password:

Notes:

Website:

URL:

Username:

Password:

Notes:

H

Website:
URL:
Username:
Password:
Notes:

Website:
URL:
Username:
Password:
Notes:

Website:
URL:
Username:
Password:
Notes:

Website:
URL:
Username:
Password:
Notes:

Website:

URL:

Username:

Password:

Notes:

Website: **H**

URL:

Username:

Password:

Notes:

Website:

URL:

Username:

Password:

Notes:

Website:

URL:

Username:

Password:

Notes:

Website:

URL:

Username:

Password:

Notes:

I

Website:

URL:

Username:

Password:

Notes:

Website:

URL:

Username:

Password:

Notes:

Website:

URL:

Username:

Password:

Notes:

Website:

URL:

Username:

Password:

Notes:

Website:

URL:

Username:

Password:

Notes:

I

Website:

URL:

Username:

Password:

Notes:

Website:

URL:

Username:

Password:

Notes:

Website:

URL:

Username:

Password:

Notes:

Website:

URL:

Username:

Password:

Notes:

Website:

URL:

Username:

Password:

Notes:

Website:

URL:

Username:

Password:

Notes:

Website:

URL:

Username:

Password:

Notes:

Website:

URL:

Username:

Password:

Notes:

Website:

URL:

Username:

Password:

Notes:

Website:

URL:

Username:

Password:

Notes:

Website:

URL:

Username:

Password:

Notes:

Website:

URL:

J

Username:

Password:

Notes:

Website:

URL:

Username:

Password:

Notes:

Website:

URL:

Username:

Password:

Notes:

Website:

URL:

Username:

Password:

Notes:

Website:

URL:

Username:

Password:

Notes:

J

Website:

URL:

Username:

Password:

Notes:

Website:

URL:

Username:

Password:

Notes:

J

Website:

URL:

Username:

Password:

Notes:

Website:

URL:

Username:

Password:

Notes:

Website:

URL:

Username:

Password:

Notes:

Website:

URL:

Username:

Password:

Notes:

Website:

URL:

Username:

Password:

Notes:

Website:

URL:

Username:

Password:

Notes:

J

Website:

URL:

Username:

Password:

Notes:

Website:

URL:

Username:

Password:

Notes:

Website:

URL:

Username:

Password:

Notes:

Website:

URL:

Username:

Password:

K   Notes:

Website:

URL:

Username:

Password:

Notes:

Website:

URL:

Username:

Password:

Notes:

Website:

URL:

Username:

Password:

Notes:

Website:

URL:

Username:

Password:

Notes:

K

Website:

URL:

Username:

Password:

Notes:

Website:

URL:

Username:

Password:

Notes:

Website:

URL:

Username:

Password:

Notes:

K

Website:

URL:

Username:

Password:

Notes:

Website:

URL:

Username:

Password:

Notes:

Website:

URL:

Username:

Password:

Notes:

Website:

URL:

Username:

Password:

Notes:

Website:

URL:

Username:

Password:

Notes:

K

Website:

URL:

Username:

Password:

Notes:

Website:

URL:

Username:

Password:

Notes:

Website:

URL:

Username:

Password:

Notes:

Website:

URL:

Username:

Password:

Notes:

L

Website:

URL:

Username:

Password:

Notes:

Website:

URL:

Username:

Password:

Notes:

Website:

URL:

Username:

Password:

Notes:

Website:

URL:

Username:

Password:

Notes:

L

Website:

URL:

Username:

Password:

Notes:

Website:

URL:

Username:

Password:

Notes:

Website:

URL:

Username:

Password:

Notes:

Website:

URL:

Username:

Password:

Notes:

L

Website:

URL:

Username:

Password:

Notes:

Website:

URL:

Username:

Password:

Notes:

Website:

URL:

Username:

Password:

Notes:

Website:

URL:

Username:

Password:

Notes:

L

Website:

URL:

Username:

Password:

Notes:

Website:

URL:

Username:

Password:

Notes:

Website:

URL:

Username:

Password:

Notes:

Website:

URL:

Username:

Password:

Notes:

M

Website:

URL:

Username:

Password:

Notes:

Website:

URL:

Username:

Password:

Notes:

Website: _____
URL: _____
Username: _____
Password: _____
Notes: _____
_____
_____
_____

Website: _____
URL: _____
Username: _____
Password: _____
Notes: _____
_____
_____
_____

M

Website: _____
URL: _____
Username: _____
Password: _____
Notes: _____
_____
_____
_____

Website: _____
URL: _____
Username: _____
Password: _____
Notes: _____
_____
_____
_____

Website:

URL:

Username:

Password:

Notes:

Website:

URL:

Username:

Password:

Notes:

M

Website:

URL:

Username:

Password:

Notes:

Website:

URL:

Username:

Password:

Notes:

Website:

URL:

Username:

Password:

Notes:

Website:

URL:

Username:

Password:

Notes:

M

Website:

URL:

Username:

Password:

Notes:

Website:

URL:

Username:

Password:

Notes:

Website:

URL:

Username:

Password:

Notes:

Website:

URL:

Username:

Password:

Notes:

N

Website:

URL:

Username:

Password:

Notes:

Website:

URL:

Username:

Password:

Notes:

Website:

URL:

Username:

Password:

Notes:

Website:

URL:

Username:

Password:

Notes:

N

Website:

URL:

Username:

Password:

Notes:

Website:

URL:

Username:

Password:

Notes:

N

Website:

URL:

Username:

Password:

Notes:

Website:

URL:

Username:

Password:

Notes:

Website:

URL:

Username:

Password:

Notes:

Website:

URL:

Username:

Password:

Notes:

Website:

URL:

Username:

Password:

Notes:

Website:

URL:

Username:

Password:

Notes:

N

Website:

URL:

Username:

Password:

Notes:

Website:

URL:

Username:

Password:

Notes:

Website:

URL:

Username:

Password:

Notes:

Website:

URL:

Username:

Password:

Notes:

O

Website:

URL:

Username:

Password:

Notes:

Website:

URL:

Username:

Password:

Notes:

Website:

URL:

Username:

Password:

Notes:

Website:

URL:

Username:

Password:

Notes:

Website:

URL:

Username:

Password:

Notes:

O

Website:

URL:

Username:

Password:

Notes:

Website:
URL:
Username:
Password:
Notes:

Website:
URL:
Username:
Password:
Notes:

O

Website:
URL:
Username:
Password:
Notes:

Website:
URL:
Username:
Password:
Notes:

Website:

URL:

Username:

Password:

Notes:

Website:

URL:

Username:

Password:

Notes:

Website:

URL:

Username:

Password:

Notes:

O

Website:

URL:

Username:

Password:

Notes:

Website:

URL:

Username:

Password:

Notes:

Website:

URL:

Username:

Password:

Notes:

P

Website:

URL:

Username:

Password:

Notes:

Website:

URL:

Username:

Password:

Notes:

Website:

URL:

Username:

Password:

Notes:

Website:

URL:

Username:

Password:

Notes:

Website:

URL:

Username:

Password:

Notes:

P

Website:

URL:

Username:

Password:

Notes:

Website:

URL:

Username:

Password:

Notes:

Website:

URL:

Username:

Password:

Notes:

P

Website:

URL:

Username:

Password:

Notes:

Website:

URL:

Username:

Password:

Notes:

Website:	
URL:	
Username:	
Password:	
Notes:	

Website:	
URL:	
Username:	
Password:	
Notes:	

Website:	
URL:	
Username:	
Password:	
Notes:	

P

Website:	
URL:	
Username:	
Password:	
Notes:	

Website:

URL:

Username:

Password:

Notes:

Website:

URL:

Username:

Password:

Notes:

Q

Website:

URL:

Username:

Password:

Notes:

Website:

URL:

Username:

Password:

Notes:

Website:

URL:

Username:

Password:

Notes:

Website:

URL:

Username:

Password:

Notes:

Website:

URL:

Username:

Password:

Notes:

Q

Website:

URL:

Username:

Password:

Notes:

Website:

URL:

Username:

Password:

Notes:

Website:

URL:

Username:

Password:

Notes:

Q

Website:

URL:

Username:

Password:

Notes:

Website:

URL:

Username:

Password:

Notes:

Website:

URL:

Username:

Password:

Notes:

Website:

URL:

Username:

Password:

Notes:

Website:

URL:

Username:

Password:

Notes:

Q

Website:

URL:

Username:

Password:

Notes:

Website:

URL:

Username:

Password:

Notes:

Website:

URL:

Username:

Password:

Notes:

Website:

URL:

Username:

Password:

Notes:

Website:

URL:

Username:

Password:

Notes:

Website:

URL:

Username:

Password:

Notes:

Website:

URL:

Username:

Password:

Notes:

Website:

URL:

Username:

Password:

Notes:

R

Website:

URL:

Username:

Password:

Notes:

Website:

URL:

Username:

Password:

Notes:

Website:

URL:

Username:

Password:

Notes:

R

Website:

URL:

Username:

Password:

Notes:

Website:

URL:

Username:

Password:

Notes:

Website:

URL:

Username:

Password:

Notes:

Website:

URL:

Username:

Password:

Notes:

Website:

URL:

Username:

Password:

Notes:

R

Website:

URL:

Username:

Password:

Notes:

Website:

URL:

Username:

Password:

Notes:

Website:

URL:

Username:

Password:

Notes:

Website:

URL:

Username:

Password:

Notes:

S

Website:

URL:

Username:

Password:

Notes:

Website:

URL:

Username:

Password:

Notes:

Website:

URL:

Username:

Password:

Notes:

Website:

URL:

Username:

Password:

Notes:

S

Website:

URL:

Username:

Password:

Notes:

Website:

URL:

Username:

Password:

Notes:

Website:

URL:

Username:

Password:

Notes:

Website:

URL:

Username:

Password:

Notes:

S

Website:

URL:

Username:

Password:

Notes:

Website:

URL:

Username:

Password:

Notes:

Website:

URL:

Username:

Password:

Notes:

Website:

URL:

Username:

Password:

Notes:

S

Website:

URL:

Username:

Password:

Notes:

Website:

URL:

Username:

Password:

Notes:

Website:

URL:

Username:

Password:

Notes:

Website:

URL:

Username:

Password:

Notes:

T

Website:

URL:

Username:

Password:

Notes:

Website:

URL:

Username:

Password:

Notes:

Website:

URL:

Username:

Password:

Notes:

Website:

URL:

Username:

Password:

Notes:

T

Website:

URL:

Username:

Password:

Notes:

Website:

URL:

Username:

Password:

Notes:

Website:

URL:

Username:

Password:

Notes:

Website:

URL:

Username:

Password:

Notes:

T

Website:

URL:

Username:

Password:

Notes:

Website:	
URL:	
Username:	
Password:	
Notes:	

Website:	
URL:	
Username:	
Password:	
Notes:	

Website:	
URL:	
Username:	
Password:	
Notes:	

T

Website:	
URL:	
Username:	
Password:	
Notes:	

Website:

URL:

Username:

Password:

Notes:

Website:

URL:

Username:

Password:

Notes:

Website:

URL:

Username:

Password:

Notes:

U

Website:

URL:

Username:

Password:

Notes:

Website:

URL:

Username:

Password:

Notes:

Website:

URL:

Username:

Password:

Notes:

Website:

URL:

Username:

Password:

Notes:

Website:

URL:

Username:

Password:

Notes:

U

Website:

URL:

Username:

Password:

Notes:

Website:

URL:

Username:

Password:

Notes:

Website:

URL:

Username:

Password:

Notes:

U

Website:

URL:

Username:

Password:

Notes:

Website:

URL:

Username:

Password:

Notes:

Website:

URL:

Username:

Password:

Notes:

Website:

URL:

Username:

Password:

Notes:

Website:

URL:

Username:

Password:

Notes:

U

Website:

URL:

Username:

Password:

Notes:

Website:

URL:

Username:

Password:

Notes:

Website:

URL:

Username:

Password:

Notes:

Website:

URL:

Username:

Password:

Notes:

V

Website:

URL:

Username:

Password:

Notes:

Website:

URL:

Username:

Password:

Notes:

Website:

URL:

Username:

Password:

Notes:

Website:

URL:

Username:

Password:

Notes:

Website:

URL:

Username:

Password:

Notes:

Website:

URL:

Username:

Password:

Notes:

Website:

URL:

Username:

Password:

Notes:

V

Website:

URL:

Username:

Password:

Notes:

Website:

URL:

Username:

Password:

Notes:

Website:

URL:

Username:

Password:

Notes:

Website:

URL:

Username:

Password:

Notes:

Website:

URL:

V

Username:

Password:

Notes:

Website:

URL:

Username:

Password:

Notes:

Website:

URL:

Username:

Password:

Notes:

Website:

URL:

Username:

Password:

Notes:

Website:

W Username:

Password:

Notes:

Website:

URL:

Username:

Password:

Notes:

Website:

URL:

Username:

Password:

Notes:

Website:

URL:

Username:

Password:

Notes:

Website:

URL:

Username:

Password:

Notes:

W

Website:

URL:

Username:

Password:

Notes:

Website:

URL:

Username:

Password:

Notes:

Website:

URL:

Username:

Password:

Notes:

Website:

URL:

W **Username:**

Password:

Notes:

Website:

URL:

Username:

Password:

Notes:

Website:

URL:

Username:

Password:

Notes:

Website:

URL:

Username:

Password:

Notes:

Website:

URL:

Username:

Password:

Notes:

W

Website:

URL:

Username:

Password:

Notes:

Website:

URL:

Username:

Password:

Notes:

Website:

URL:

Username:

Password:

Notes:

X

Website:

URL:

Username:

Password:

Notes:

Website:

URL:

Username:

Password:

Notes:

Website:

URL:

Username:

Password:

Notes:

Website:

URL:

Username:

Password:

Notes:

Website:

URL:

Username:

Password:

Notes:

X

Website:

URL:

Username:

Password:

Notes:

Website:

URL:

Username:

Password:

Notes:

Website:

URL:

Username:

Password:

Notes:

Website:

URL:

Username:

Password:

Notes:

X

Website:

URL:

Username:

Password:

Notes:

Website:

URL:

Username:

Password:

Notes:

Website:

URL:

Username:

Password:

Notes:

Website:

URL:

Username:

Password:

Notes:

X

Website:

URL:

Username:

Password:

Notes:

Website:

URL:

Username:

Password:

Notes:

Website:

URL:

Username:

Password:

Notes:

Website:

URL:

Username:

Password:

Notes:

Y

Website:

URL:

Username:

Password:

Notes:

Website:

URL:

Username:

Password:

Notes:

Website:

URL:

Username:

Password:

Notes:

Website:

URL:

Username:

Password:

Notes:

Website:

URL:

Username:

Password:

Notes:

Website:

URL:

Username:

Password:

Notes:

Website:

URL:

Username:

Password:

Notes:

Website:

URL:

Username:

Password:

Notes:

Y

Website:

URL:

Username:

Password:

Notes:

Website:

URL:

Username:

Password:

Notes:

Website:

URL:

Username:

Password:

Notes:

Website:

URL:

Username:

Password:

Notes:

Y

Website:
URL:
Username:
Password:
Notes:

Website:
URL:
Username:
Password:
Notes:

Website:
URL:
Username:
Password:
Notes:

Website:
URL:
Username:
Password:
Notes:

Z

Website:

URL:

Username:

Password:

Notes:

Website:

URL:

Username:

Password:

Notes:

Website:

URL:

Username:

Password:

Notes:

Website:

URL:

Username:

Password:

Notes:

Z

Website:

URL:

Username:

Password:

Notes:

Website:

URL:

Username:

Password:

Notes:

Website:

URL:

Username:

Password:

Notes:

Website:

URL:

Username:

Password:

Notes:

Z

Website:

URL:

Username:

Password:

Notes:

Website:

URL:

Username:

Password:

Notes:

Website:

URL:

Username:

Password:

Notes:

Website:

URL:

Username:

Password:

Notes:

Z

Website:

URL:

Username:

Password:

Notes:

Website:

URL:

Username:

Password:

Notes:

Website:

URL:

Username:

Password:

Notes:

Website:

URL:

Username:

Password:

Notes:

Website:

URL:

Username:

Password:

Notes:

Website:

URL:

Username:

Password:

Notes:

Website:

URL:

Username:

Password:

Notes:

Website:

URL:

Username:

Password:

Notes:

Website:

URL:

Username:

Password:

Notes:

Website:

URL:

Username:

Password:

Notes:

Website:

URL:

Username:

Password:

Notes:

Website:

URL:

Username:

Password:

Notes:

Website:

URL:

Username:

Password:

Notes:

Website:

URL:

Username:

Password:

Notes:

Website:

URL:

Username:

Password:

Notes:

Website:

URL:

Username:

Password:

Notes:

www.ingramcontent.com/pod-product-compliance
Lightning Source LLC
Chambersburg PA
CBHW070604220526
45467CB00003B/1284